"I Am for Equal Rights"

Sojourner Truth Fights for Equal Rights

Frances E. Ruffin

ROSEN CLASSROOM
PRIMARYSOURCE
Rosen Classroom Books & Materials™
New York

Published in 2004 by The Rosen Publishing Group, Inc.
29 East 21st Street, New York, NY 10010

Editor: Jennifer Silate
Book Design: Christopher Logan
Photo researcher: Rebecca Anguin-Cohen
Series photo researcher: Jeff Wendt

Photo Credits: Cover (left), title page, pp. 14, 18, 22, 29, 30, 31, 32 Courtesy of the archives of the Historical Society of Battle Creek; cover (right) illustration © Debra Wainwright/The Rosen Publishing Group; p. 6 Historic Northampton, Northampton, Massachusetts; p. 10 Cindy Reiman

ISBN: 0-8239-4388-7
6-pack ISBN: 0-8239-4389-5

Manufactured in the United States of America

Contents

	Preface	4
1	A Broken Promise	7
2	Freedom	11
3	Victory!	15
4	The Narrative	19
5	Fighting to the End	23
	Glossary	27
	Primary Sources	28

Preface

Sojourner Truth was born in New York, around 1797. She was a slave. Her name then was Isabella. Her master was a hotel owner named Charles Ardinburgh. Isabella lived with her mother Betsy, her father James, and her brother Peter. They lived with ten other slaves in a dark cellar under the hotel her master owned. Life as a slave was very hard. Slaves did not have any rights. They were the property of their masters. Slaves were often beaten when their masters were angry with them. Most slaves were not allowed to learn to read or write. Slave owners even decided whom their slaves would marry.

Isabella was nine years old when her first master died. Isabella was sold to a farmer named John Neely. Neely bought Isabella and some sheep for $100. Isabella would have two more masters before she was finally free.

Isabella's fourth master was John Dumont, another farmer in New York. About 1815, Dumont wanted Isabella to marry and have children. Isabella was forced to marry Thomas, an older slave who also lived on Dumont's farm. Isabella had five children, four girls and one boy.

In 1826, Isabella ran away from her owners. She was only able to take her baby, Sophia, with her. The rest of her children remained slaves. Once free, Isabella changed her name to Sojourner Truth. Truth started speaking out against slavery. She also spoke in favor of women's rights. She thought that African Americans and all women should have the same rights as white men.

In the late 1840s, Sojourner Truth sat with a friend named Olive Gilbert. She wanted to tell Gilbert the story of her life. Truth could neither read nor write, but she knew that she had an important story to tell....

This picture, done in the late 1800s, shows Truth hard at work. As a slave, Sojourner Truth was forced to do long hours of hard work without pay.

Chapter One

A Broken Promise

On a cold winter's day in 1847, Sojourner Truth sat with her friend, Olive Gilbert. Truth was about fifty years old. She was dressed in a simple, dark-gray dress. She gave Gilbert a cup of tea. Truth pulled a white shawl around her shoulders before she spoke.

"You asked me to tell you about how I got my freedom," Truth said as she leaned back in her chair to begin her story. "Well, I had been given a promise that I would be set free. That promise was made to me in 1824.

"I had finished my work in the fields. I saw my master, John Dumont, watching me and the other slaves. I went up to him and I said, 'Good evening, Mr. Dumont. May I speak with you about something important?'

"'All right, I have a few minutes,' Dumont replied. I gathered up my courage and said to him, 'I've heard that the laws will be changed. Slaves in New York will be free on July 4, 1827.' 'Only the ones over twenty-eight years old,' he said. 'Well, I am older than that now. So, will I be free?' I asked him.

"He said that I was right. And do you know what he said after that? He asked me if I would be willing to work harder for the next two years in return for being freed a year earlier."

"What did you say?" Gilbert asked.

"I said yes," answered Truth. "I said yes, and I almost cried I was so happy. I worked hard for the next couple of months, but then I hurt my hand. It was horrible. My hand never healed right." She held up her twisted hand.

"I didn't give up, though," Truth continued. "I kept working. I did whatever I could with my hand. I worked all day and night.

"When July 4, 1826 came, Mr. Dumont would not give me my freedom. He said that I did not do everything in our agreement. I did not accept this. I did everything I could and more. He was being unfair. I did my usual work and even wove about one hundred pounds of wool into yarn. I figured that settled our agreement. Then, I left."

"You mean that you ran away," said Gilbert.

"I **took** my freedom," said Truth. "It was December. I could not take all of my children with me. I took Sophia, my youngest. She was not even one year old yet. I kissed the others as they slept. It was so hard to leave them. It was so cold that the frozen ground crunched beneath my feet. I walked off of that farm and I never looked back."

A sign outside the courthouse where Sojourner Truth's case was held tells about the famous trial.

Chapter Two

Freedom

"Truth, where did you go when you left Dumont?" Gilbert asked.

Sojourner Truth poured Olive Gilbert another cup of tea. She looked over at her friend who was writing in a cloth-covered book. "I walked until I reached an old farmer's house and begged for shelter for me and my baby," she answered. "He told me about a Quaker couple named Van Wagener who lived nearby. They invited me to stay with them in their home.

"Soon, though, Dumont found out where I had gone," Truth said, looking out the window at the falling snow. "He ordered Isaac Van Wagener to give me and my poor baby back to him. We were still his property, he said. But then, something wonderful happened. Isaac Van Wagener offered to pay

Dumont twenty dollars for me and five dollars for Sophia. Dumont just took the money and left.

"Mr. Van Wagener told me that I was free! He said that I could work for him and that he would pay me," Truth said with a smile. "That was my first job as a free woman.

"I wasn't happy for very long, though." Truth shook her head. "I heard that my boy, Peter, had been sold to a man named Fowler, in Alabama. Peter was only six years old. There were no laws freeing the slaves in Alabama, you know. If I didn't do anything, he was going to be a slave for his whole life!"

"What did you do, Sojourner?" asked Gilbert.

"First, I went to the Dumonts' house," said Truth. "I pleaded with Mrs. Dumont to get my boy back, but she didn't care. She didn't think he was worth all of the fuss. I talked to everyone I could. No one cared about Peter. He was just another slave boy to them. Finally, I went to the Quakers. Quakers had always been so kind to me. I thought that one of them might help. And you know what? Two helped—two lawyers. They said it was illegal to sell a slave from New York to someone in another state. They helped me take Fowler to court."

"Was that difficult?" asked Gilbert as she wrote what Truth had said.

"Yes, it sure was. It took an entire year to get Fowler and my boy to come to New York for the trial," responded Truth. "When I saw my boy in the courtroom, my eyes filled with tears. He looked bad."

"Did the man beat him?" asked Gilbert.

"He did. Peter had a large scar on his forehead that wasn't there when I left him at Dumont's," answered Truth.

"So, Truth, what happened during the trial?" asked Gilbert.

"It was awful. Peter held onto Fowler and yelled, 'She's not my mother!' That broke my heart." A tear rolled down Sojourner's cheek. "My boy disowned me!"

Sojourner Truth used ads like this one to tell people when she was giving a speech.

Chapter Three

Victory!

"Oh no! Fowler must have told him to say that. How can a boy disown his mother?" asked Gilbert.

"I think that nasty Fowler told him I was a monster," answered Truth. "The poor little boy didn't know what to believe. The judge knew that I was his mother, though. He said, 'This child will be given to his mother. He will have no other master but his mother.' After that, Peter was mine."

"That's amazing, Sojourner," said Gilbert, writing quickly to get everything in her notebook. "You must have given so much hope to other slaves."

"I was told that I was the first slave to get back her child who was sold," replied Truth. "Most slaves who are wronged do not get to go to court. I was lucky to have the help of so many people.

No parent should have to go through that. It was horrible."

"Oh, my friend! You have been through so much. Your story is really going to help people see how wrong slavery is," Gilbert said.

When she had finished writing about Truth's court case, Gilbert laid down her pen. "Truth, tell me how you started calling yourself Sojourner Truth? That wasn't your name when you were a slave, right?" she asked.

"That's right, my name was just Isabella, until about three years ago. At the time, I was working as a housekeeper in New York City," Truth replied. "One day, I decided it was time to leave. I had more important work to do. I packed a pillowcase with my clothes and about twenty-five cents. Then, I walked to a boat that took me to Brooklyn. From there, I began to walk toward the east.

"I walked through Long Island, New York. I was truly free. In the evenings, I spoke at religious camp meetings that were held there. I started thinking about my name. Isabella was a slave's name. I was no longer a slave. I decided that I needed a new name to go with my new freedom. I chose Sojourner because it means traveler. I chose Truth because I speak the truth. As a free woman, I travel the country, speaking the truth to whomever will listen. That is why my name is Sojourner Truth."

Truth stared at her hands. "Do you have everything you need for the book?" she asked Gilbert.

"I think so," answered Gilbert as she closed the notebook. "What do you plan to do once the book is finished?"

"Oh, I think that it is time for me to pack my bags again," Truth told Gilbert. "I need to talk to the people of America."

In her lifetime, Sojourner Truth met many great people including President Abraham Lincoln (shown above).

Chapter Four

The Narrative

The **Narrative of Sojourner Truth** was printed in 1850. Truth traveled around the country. She gave many speeches against slavery and for women's rights. She sold her book for twenty-five cents each. She used the money she made from selling her book to buy a house in Battle Creek, Michigan. While living in Battle Creek, Sojourner Truth met Frances Titus. The two became great friends and traveled together from time to time. In late 1874, Sojourner Truth paid a visit to her friend's house.

"Who is it?" a voice called from inside the house when Truth knocked on the door.

"It is Sojourner Truth."

Frances Titus opened the door to greet Truth.

"How are you, my friend?" she asked as she hugged Truth.

"I'm doing well, Frances," answered Truth. "How are you today?"

"Very well, thank you. Please come in," said Titus.

"Frances, I have come to ask a favor of you," Truth said as she sat down in Titus's living room.

Frances Titus joined her friend on the sofa. "What can I do for you, Sojourner?" she asked.

"I am getting older, Frances, and I would like to add my "Book of Life" to the **Narrative**. It will be nice to have something to tell about my life since the **Narrative** was written. Besides, I plan to go to the one-hundred-year celebration of the Unites States of America, in Philadelphia, in 1876. I would like to be able to sell a new book there. Perhaps I could make some money so that I can take care of myself when I am too old to travel, which I fear will be very soon. Will you help me add to my book?"

"Of course I will help you, Sojourner," replied Titus.

Sojourner Truth held in her hands a large book, bursting with papers. Sojourner handed her "Book of Life" to her friend. "Inside this book are notes from many of the wonderful people I have met. There are also clippings from the newspapers of many of the towns where I have been," she said.

"There is a lot here, Sojourner," said Titus, opening the book to read some of the notes inside it. "Look at all of the wonderful signatures you have collected. Here is one from President Abraham Lincoln!"

Sojourner smiled and said, "President Lincoln was a fine man. It has been ten years since I met him. He treated me with such kindness. He even called me 'Aunty.'"

"That will make a great story for your book! What other good things have you got in here?" asked Titus as she studied Truth's book.

Sojourner Truth dressed simply her entire life. She often wore a plain dress with a white shawl.

Chapter Five

Fighting to the End

"You have so many signatures of famous workers for women's rights: Lucretia Mott, Harriet Beecher Stowe, Susan B. Anthony. Are you still in touch with these people?" asked Titus.

"I haven't seen them in some time. My work with them is still not done, though. Women still cannot vote," responded Truth.

"They have all written some wonderful things about you, Sojourner. This article by a Mrs. Francis Gage is about a speech you made at a meeting for women's rights in 1851," said Titus. She was reading a yellowed piece of newspaper from Truth's "Book of Life."

"She writes that you were booed by some people there. They did not want you to mix your fight against slavery with the fight for women's rights," continued Titus.

"Some people didn't think that white people would be interested in women's rights if black people's rights were talked about, too. Some yelled at me, some cursed. I just stood up for the truth. I remember telling them, 'I could work and eat as much as a man.' That's the truth!" said Truth with a smile.

Frances Titus nodded. "Here is something from a Mr. John Eaton, Jr. about your work with the Freedmen's Bureau," she said.

"Mr. Eaton helped me to get a job with the Freedmen's hospital. I helped the men who had been freed from slavery after it was made illegal in 1865," Truth told her.

"Was that during the time you spent in Washington, D.C.?" asked Titus.

"Yes," said Truth. "You know, when I first got to Washington, D.C., it was still legal for streetcars to make the black people sit in a different car. They changed the law in 1865, but people didn't change. Once, I wanted to ride a streetcar with Ms. Laura Haviland, to go to the Freedmen's hospital. When I tried to get on, the conductor grabbed me by the arm and tried to throw me from the car. Ms. Haviland tried to help me, and the man said, 'Does she belong to you? You better get her off this car!'"

"What did you do, Sojourner?" asked Titus.

"The conductor eventually let us on the car, but a bone in my shoulder was injured. The Freedmen's Bureau helped me to get a lawyer. I was back in court before I knew it," said Truth.

"Did you win your case?" asked Titus.

"Yes, I did. That conductor lost his job! It caused quite a stir, too. People all over the city were talking about it. Soon, the streetcars were loaded with black and white people together. It was beautiful!" said Truth.

"What a wonderful story!" Titus exclaimed. "Do you mind if I put that in the book?"

"Not at all. I'm proud of that," answered Truth, smiling.

Sojourner Truth looked out the window at the setting sun. "It's getting late," she said. "I must go now. Thank you so much for helping me with my book." Sojourner Truth rose from her seat and hugged her friend.

"I will see you soon," Titus said as she walked Truth to the door.

Frances Titus finished her work on Sojourner Truth's "Book of Life" by the end of 1884. In 1875, Titus borrowed $350 to print five thousand copies of the **Narrative of Sojourner Truth** with the "Book of Life" added to it. Sojourner Truth was eager to repay her friend. She fell ill, however, and never made it to Philadelphia where she had hoped to sell the books. Truth's health improved over the next couple of years and she was able to travel again. She made speeches around the country for women's rights. Truth's good health did not last for long. She died on November 26, 1883. Frances Titus added another chapter to Sojourner Truth's book in 1884 to remember all of the things that Truth did in her life. Today, Sojourner Truth is still remembered for her life-long fight for equal rights.

Glossary

celebration (sel-uh-BRAY-shuhn) a joyous ceremony or gathering, usually to mark a major event

conductor (kuhn-DUK-tur) someone who operates a streetcar, bus, or train

disown (diss-OHN) to refuse to accept someone as a relative

Freedmen's Bureau (FREED-menz BYUR-oh) an organization set up in 1865 to help freed slaves

lawyer (LAW-yur) a person who is trained to advise people about the law and who acts and speaks for them in court

Quaker (KWAY-kur) a member of the Society of Friends, a Christian group founded in 1650 that prefers simple religious services and opposes war

religious (ri-LIJ-uhs) having to do with a specific system of belief, faith, and worship

scar (SKAR) a mark left on your skin by a cut or wound that has healed

shelter (SHEL-tur) a place where you can keep covered in bad weather or stay safe and protected from danger

signature (SIG-nuh-chur) the individual way someone writes his or her name, usually in script

Primary Sources

Letters, diaries, photographs, maps, and other materials that were done by people long ago can tell us about history. We know much about Sojourner Truth's life because she recorded her stories in her book the **Narrative of Sojourner Truth**. From the stories she told her friend Olive Gilbert, readers learn what her early life was like.

The "Book of Life" helps us to understand how Sojourner Truth affected the world around her. It contains newspaper stories and letters written by many people. By analyzing these writings, we can learn what others thought of Truth's actions, beliefs, and speeches.

Other sources, such as the objects she used, also give us a look into the world of Sojourner Truth. For example, upon evaluating her signature on page 32, we can understand how Truth struggled to sign her own name. Sources such as these give us an idea of what life was like for Sojourner Truth.

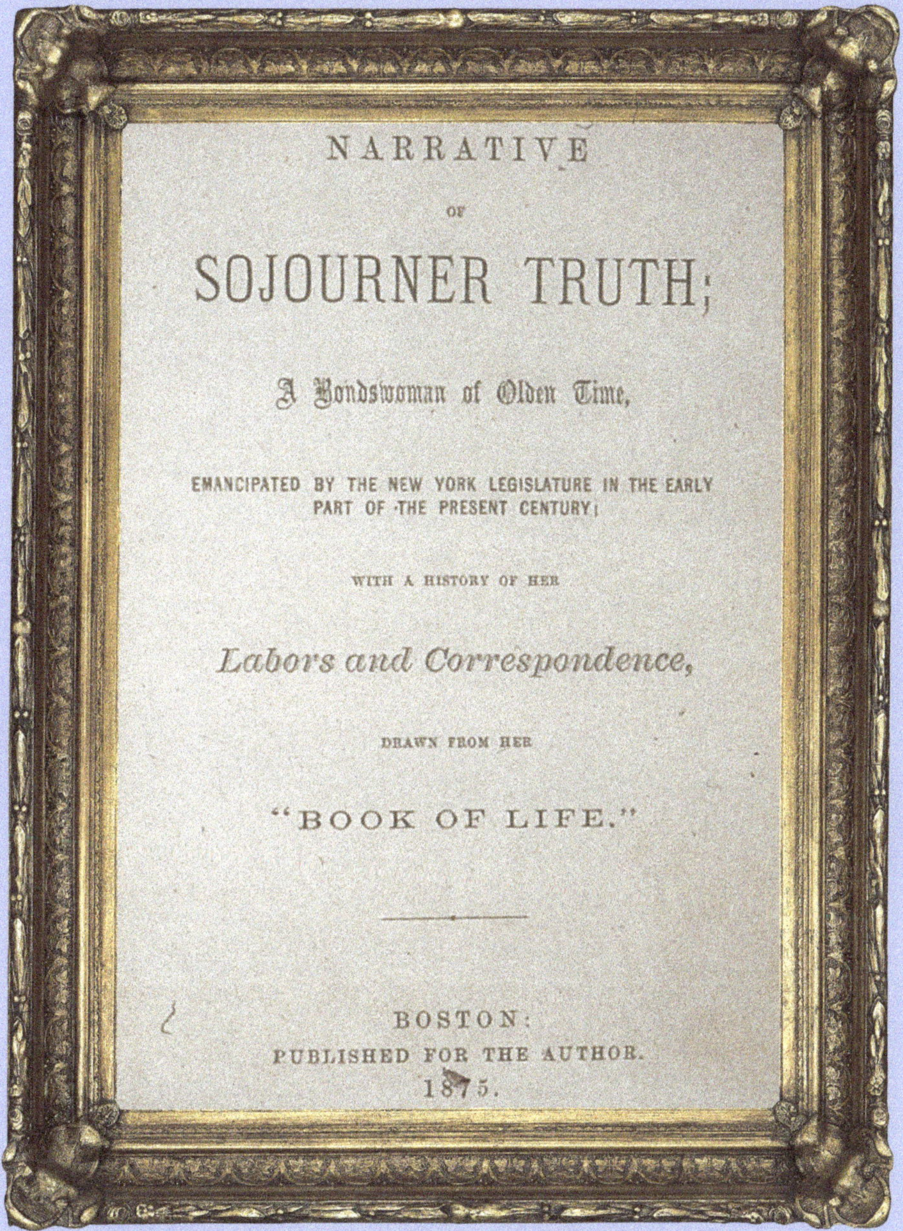

NARRATIVE

OF

SOJOURNER TRUTH;

A Bondswoman of Olden Time,

EMANCIPATED BY THE NEW YORK LEGISLATURE IN THE EARLY PART OF THE PRESENT CENTURY;

WITH A HISTORY OF HER

Labors and Correspondence,

DRAWN FROM HER

"BOOK OF LIFE."

BOSTON:
PUBLISHED FOR THE AUTHOR.
1875.

The **Narrative of Sojourner Truth** was printed many times over the years. This title page is from an 1875 printing. It included the "Book of Life."

Sojourner Truth's oldest child Diana (shown above) was born around 1815. She lived with Truth in Michigan.

Sojourner stood behind this podium to give speeches in a church in Michigan.

Though she was a great speaker, Sojourner Truth could not read or write. This is Truth's only known signature.